I0049145

From Leadership To Success

The Timeless Laws

Wisdoms From 2000 Years Ago

SuShu (素书) - Huang Shi Gong

Translated By: Morning Lee

© WealthDao Investing and Consulting, Morning Lee.

Author:
Huang Shi Gong - around Qin and Han Dynasty 2000 years ago

Translator: Morning Lee

WealthDao Investing and Consulting
PO BOX 83008 Kingsway
Burnaby BC Canada V5H0A4
www.WealthDaoinc.com

More information about this book
www.RiskFreeStartup.com
Youtube & Tiktok: @RiskFreeStartup
Instagram & Facebook: RiskFreeStartup

Table of Contents

Prologue: The Path to Wisdom and Success

The Student: Zhang Liang

Guided by the principles of *Su Shu*, Zhang Liang became one of the most revered strategists of the Han Dynasty, serving as the most important advisor to Liu Bang, the founder of the dynasty. His wisdom and cunning, shaped by the teachings of Huang Shi Gong, played a pivotal role in the eventual overthrow of the Qin Dynasty and the establishment of a new era.

His genius lay not only in his military strategies but also in his ability to read people, navigate complex situations, and ensure long-term success. Zhang Liang's legendary encounter with an old man at Yi Bridge is one of the most iconic examples of how a single moment of wisdom can transform a life.

The Story of Zhang Liang and the Yellow Rock Old Man (Translated from Records of the Grand Historian) Zhang Liang was originally from the ancient state of Han. One day, while leisurely walking near Yi Bridge in Xiapi, he encountered an old man dressed in coarse clothing. The man approached Zhang Liang, deliberately dropped his shoe off the bridge, and turned to Zhang Liang, saying, "Young man, go fetch my shoe!"

Zhang Liang, startled and insulted by the audacity of the old man, initially wanted to retaliate. However, out of respect for his age, he restrained himself, climbed down the bridge, and retrieved the shoe. The old man then said, "Put it on for me!" Zhang Liang, suppressing his anger, knelt down and helped the man put on the shoe. The old man laughed and left.

Astonished by the encounter, Zhang Liang watched him intently as he walked away. After traveling about a mile, the old man returned and said, "You are teachable. Meet me here at dawn in five days."

Curious and intrigued, Zhang Liang agreed. Five days later, Zhang Liang arrived at the appointed time, only to find the old man already there. The old man scolded him, "You are late to meet an elder! Return in another five days and come earlier."

Zhang Liang, feeling both humbled and determined, came again in five days, this time at the first crow of the rooster. Yet again, the old man had arrived before him. Angered, the man exclaimed, "Late again! Come earlier in another five days."

On the final attempt, Zhang Liang arrived in the middle of the night, well before the agreed time. At last, the old man smiled and said, "This is how one must act." He then handed Zhang Liang a book, saying, "Study this, and you will become a teacher of kings. In ten years, you will rise to greatness. In thirteen years, you will see me again beneath the Yellow Stone Mountain in Jibei."

The old man disappeared after this cryptic message. When Zhang Liang examined the book, he found it was the *Art of War by Taigong*. Zhang Liang found it extraordinary and frequently practiced and recited it.

The *Records of the Grand Historian* explicitly states that the old man, later known as the "Yellow Rock Old Man," gave Zhang Liang the *Taigong Bingfa*. However, there is debate surrounding this text. One school of thought believes the *Taigong Bingfa* might actually be the *Sushu*. Others argue that the *Sushu* is a later forgery, attributed to Zhang Shangying during the Song dynasty.

Regardless of its authorship, the contents of the *Sushu* are undoubtedly profound and valuable. Its principles hold timeless wisdom, offering insights that remain relevant even today. The philosophies and strategies within provide lessons on leadership, ethics, and decision-making–teachings that can guide us in both personal and professional pursuits.

True to the old man's prophecy, Zhang Liang diligently studied the book's teachings, reciting and mastering its principles. Over time, his wisdom and strategies helped him become one of the most influential tacticians in Chinese history, proving that the lessons he learned transcended the pages of any single text.

Original Chapter One

Translation

The Way, Virtue, Benevolence, Righteousness, and Propriety are five aspects that form a unified whole.

The Way （Dao） is the path that people follow, allowing all things to progress without understanding their origin.

Virtue （De） is what people attain, enabling all things to obtain their desired fulfillment.

Benevolence （Ren） is what connects people, embodying compassion and empathy, nurturing life and growth.

Righteousness （Yi） is what people should adhere to, rewarding good and punishing evil, establishing accomplishments and affairs.

Propriety （Li） is what people practice, rising early and retiring late, to establish the order of human relations.
For one to truly understand human essence, none of these aspects can be absent.

The virtuous and wise clearly comprehend the cycles of prosperity and decline, the patterns of success and failure, the dynamics of order and chaos, and the principles of departure and return. Thus, they remain hidden, embracing the Way and waiting for the right moment.

When the moment comes, they act, excelling in their roles. They seize opportunities to accomplish unparalleled achievements.

If the moment does not come, they quietly end their lives.
Therefore, their principles are lofty, and

their names endure through generations.

Summary of Chapter One:

Original Principles

The first chapter introduces the foundational concepts of **The Way (Dao)**, **Virtue (De)**, **Benevolence (Ren)**, **Righteousness (Yi)**, and **Propriety (Li)**, emphasizing their interconnectedness as essential elements for understanding the human condition and achieving harmony in life and society.

1.   The Five Pillars of Harmony:

The Way (Dao): Represents the universal path that governs all existence. It allows everything to progress naturally, even if its origins remain unknowable.

Virtue (De): Refers to the ability to attain what is needed for fulfillment and growth, enabling both individuals and all things to achieve their potential.

Benevolence (Ren): Embodies compassion and empathy, nurturing life and fostering connections between people.

Righteousness (Yi): Enforces justice by rewarding good and punishing evil, ensuring fairness and order in society.

Propriety (Li): Establishes social order through discipline and proper conduct, guiding human interactions and relationships.

2. The Essence of Understanding:

To fully comprehend the human experience, all five elements must be present and integrated. They form a comprehensive framework for navigating life's complexities and achieving a balanced existence.

3. The Wisdom of the Virtuous:

The chapter highlights the perspective of the wise, who observe and understand the cycles of prosperity and decline, success and failure, order and chaos, and beginnings and endings.

Such individuals align themselves with the Way, knowing when to act and when to remain hidden. They embrace patience, waiting for the right moment to seize opportunities for extraordinary accomplishments.

4. The Legacy of the Wise:

When the timing aligns with their principles, the virtuous act decisively, achieving greatness that leaves a lasting legacy. Conversely, if circumstances do not permit action, they quietly retreat, maintaining their integrity and principles.

Their adherence to these lofty ideals ensures their names are remembered and respected through generations.

Central Message

Chapter One establishes a philosophical foundation for living a virtuous and impactful life. It teaches that true wisdom lies in understanding the universal laws, acting with compassion and justice, and following proper conduct. The virtuous wait patiently for the right moment, achieving greatness while remaining aligned with the Way. Through this balance of action and restraint, they leave a legacy that endures beyond their time.

Samples

In this chapter 1, we explore the foundational concepts of The Way (Dao), Virtue (De), Benevolence (Ren), Righteousness (Yi), and Propriety (Li) through real-life examples. These principles, though ancient, are vividly illustrated in the actions and legacies of notable figures and organizations from both history and contemporary times. These samples not only bring the philosophical concepts to life but also demonstrate their relevance and application in modern society, inspiring readers to incorporate these timeless values into their own lives and leadership practices.

1. **The Way (Dao) - Elon Musk and SpaceX**: Elon Musk's approach with SpaceX exemplifies the principle of the 'Way' by adhering to a profound, visionary goal of making human life multi-planetary. This overarching

mission guides all strategic decisions, technological developments, and partnerships, showcasing a steadfast commitment to a visionary path, even in the face of immense challenges and skepticism.

2. **Virtue (De) - Mother Teresa**: Mother Teresa represented 'Virtue' through her unwavering dedication to serving those in dire need. Her establishment of the Missionaries of Charity and her life's work in aiding the sick, poor, and dying in Kolkata and globally highlight how true fulfillment can arise from selfless service and profound compassion, leaving an enduring impact on the world.

3. **Benevolence (Ren) - Tony Hsieh of Zappos**: Tony Hsieh at Zappos championed 'Benevolence' by prioritizing corporate culture and employee well-being. His

leadership transformed Zappos into a model of how fostering a compassionate and supportive work environment leads to business success and high employee morale, illustrating the practical benefits of nurturing life and growth within a corporate context.

4. **Righteousness (Yi) - Howard Schultz and Starbucks**: Howard Schultz of Starbucks demonstrated 'Righteousness' by implementing policies that significantly benefited his employees, such as offering health insurance to part-time workers and investing in educational opportunities for staff. These actions, guided by a sense of justice and fairness, helped establish Starbucks as a leader in ethical corporate practices.

5. **Propriety (Li) - IBM's Corporate Culture**: IBM has long been celebrated for its strong emphasis on 'Propriety' in its corporate culture. The company's adherence to strict dress codes, professional conduct, and disciplined work processes has set standards within the tech industry, promoting a formal yet respectful atmosphere that facilitates order and respect among employees and towards clients.

These examples not only breathe life into ancient teachings but also serve as guides on how we can apply these principles to achieve personal and professional excellence today.

Correctness of the Way Chapter Two

Translation

Virtue that is sufficient to inspire distant lands,

Faith that is strong enough to unify differences,

Righteousness that earns the hearts of the people,

Talent that understands the lessons of history,

Clarity that illuminates those below—

These are the hallmarks of an exceptional individual.

Conduct that serves as a model for others,

Wisdom that resolves doubts and uncertainties,

Trustworthiness that ensures adherence to agreements,

Integrity that enables equitable distribution of wealth—

These are the marks of a remarkable leader.

To steadfastly fulfill one's duties without neglect,

To uphold righteousness without wavering,

To endure suspicion without compromising integrity,

To encounter profit without succumbing to greed–

These are the characteristics of an extraordinary person.

Summary of Chapter Two:

Correctness of the Way

This chapter outlines the attributes and principles that define exceptional individuals, remarkable leaders, and extraordinary people. It emphasizes the importance of virtues, actions, and character in aligning with the Way (Dao) to inspire, lead, and succeed.

1. The Hallmarks of Exceptional Individuals:

Virtue that inspires even distant lands, faith that unifies diversity, and righteousness that wins the people's loyalty.

Talent grounded in historical understanding and clarity that guides those below are essential qualities of individuals who stand out.

2. The Qualities of Remarkable Leaders:

Leaders must lead by example, resolve doubts with wisdom, honor agreements with trustworthiness, and ensure equitable distribution of resources with integrity.

These traits enable leaders to gain the respect and loyalty of their followers while fostering a harmonious and just society.

3. The Characteristics of Extraordinary People:

They consistently fulfill their responsibilities, remain unwavering in righteousness, endure suspicion without losing their integrity, and resist greed in the face of profit.

These qualities embody the resilience, moral strength, and steadfastness that distinguish extraordinary individuals from others.

Central Message

Chapter Two highlights the moral and practical dimensions of greatness, focusing on the alignment of virtues, wisdom, and integrity. Whether as individuals or leaders, those who embody these principles can inspire others, resolve challenges, and build trust. By steadfastly adhering to righteousness and resisting temptations, they achieve harmony with the Way and leave a profound impact on the world.

Samples

Chapter 2, "Correctness of the Way," outlines the attributes essential for exceptional leadership and moral character. To vividly illustrate these attributes, this section features examples from both the corporate world and historical figures, demonstrating how virtues such as integrity, trustworthiness, and righteousness are pivotal in shaping influential and admirable leaders.

1. **Virtue Inspiring Distant Lands - Nelson Mandela**: Nelson Mandela's leadership exemplifies virtue that inspired not only his nation but also the world. His dedication to justice and reconciliation in post-apartheid South Africa showcases how true virtue can bridge vast divides and inspire a global audience.

2. **Faith Unifying Diversity - Malala Yousafzai**: Malala Yousafzai stands as a beacon of faith in the power of education for girls worldwide despite cultural and violent opposition. Her

steadfast belief and advocacy have unified people across diverse geographies and ideologies to support the right to education for all children.

3. **Righteousness Earning Hearts - Abraham Lincoln**: Abraham Lincoln's commitment to righteousness during the American Civil War, particularly his efforts to end slavery and preserve the Union, helped him earn the lasting respect and admiration of his people, demonstrating how righteousness can indeed win the hearts of many.

4. **Talent Understanding History - Steve Jobs**: Steve Jobs' ability to draw on historical lessons in technology and design led to revolutionary products like the iPhone and iPad. His talent for understanding the lessons of

technological history enabled Apple to innovate and dominate the market.

5. **Clarity Illuminating the Path - Indra Nooyi of PepsiCo**: Indra Nooyi, former CEO of PepsiCo, provided clear leadership that transformed the company with initiatives like the "Performance with Purpose" strategy. Her clarity in vision and strategy illuminated the path for PepsiCo's transformation into a more sustainable and profitable company.

These examples provide tangible insights into how the virtues described in Chapter 2 can be manifested in leadership and personal conduct, offering readers models of how they might apply these principles in their own lives and careers.

Cultivating Aspirations Chapter Three

Translation

Eliminating excessive desires is the way to rid oneself of burdens.

Restraining improper thoughts and curbing evil actions is the way to prevent mistakes.

Avoiding overindulgence in alcohol and abstaining from lust are the ways to remain untainted.

Steering clear of suspicion and staying away from doubtful situations are the ways to avoid errors.

Broadening knowledge through extensive learning and asking thoughtful questions is the way to expand understanding.

Living with high moral conduct and speaking with subtlety is the way to refine one's character.

Practicing humility, frugality, and restraint is the way to maintain self-discipline.

Planning deeply and considering the future is the way to avoid hardship.

Being close to benevolent and upright friends is the way to gain support during adversity.

Adopting tolerance and sincerity in one's actions is the way to connect with others.

Appointing capable individuals and utilizing their talents is the way to accomplish tasks.

Eliminating hatred and rejecting slander is the way to prevent chaos.

Drawing lessons from the past and applying them to the present is the way to avoid confusion.

Measuring twice before taking action is the way to respond effectively to urgent situations.

Using adaptability and wisdom to handle changes is the way to untangle complications.

Knowing when to withdraw and act prudently is the way to remain faultless.

Diligence and perseverance are the ways to achieve success.

Maintaining an upright and virtuous character is the way to secure lasting peace.

Summary of Chapter Three:

Cultivating Aspirations

This chapter emphasizes the cultivation of virtues, discipline, and wisdom as the foundation for personal growth, success, and harmonious relationships. It provides a detailed guide on how to refine one's character, navigate challenges, and achieve aspirations.

1.   Eliminating Burdens and Mistakes:

Freeing oneself from excessive desires reduces unnecessary burdens.

Restraining improper thoughts, curbing harmful actions, and avoiding indulgence in alcohol or lust ensure a life free from corruption and errors.

2.   Cultivating Knowledge and Character:

Expanding understanding through learning and thoughtful questioning broadens one's perspective.

Living with high moral standards, practicing humility and restraint, and speaking with subtlety refine one's character and enhance self-discipline.

3. Building Relationships and Accomplishing Goals:

Maintaining benevolent and upright friendships provides support in adversity.

Tolerance, sincerity, and appointing capable individuals foster strong connections and enable the accomplishment of meaningful tasks.

4. Avoiding Chaos and Confusion:

Rejecting hatred and slander prevents chaos, while drawing lessons from the past and applying them to the present ensures clarity.

Measuring decisions carefully before acting and using wisdom to adapt to changes allows for effective responses to challenges.

5. Achieving Success and Lasting Peace:

Diligence, perseverance, and prudent withdrawal ensure long-term success.

Upholding an upright and virtuous character leads to enduring peace and fulfillment.

Central Message

Chapter Three provides a comprehensive framework for self-cultivation and success, emphasizing the importance of discipline, learning, and relationships. It advocates for a balanced approach to life—one that combines moral integrity, thoughtful planning, and adaptability to achieve aspirations and maintain harmony.

Samples

In "Cultivating Aspirations," we explore the importance of self-discipline, restraint, and continuous learning as key to achieving one's personal and professional goals. This section will highlight examples from various fields, demonstrating how these virtues are applied by successful individuals and organizations to foster growth, success, and ethical conduct.

1. **Eliminating Excessive Desires - Warren Buffett**: Warren Buffett is renowned for his frugal lifestyle despite his immense wealth. His ability to eliminate excessive desires and focus on what truly matters has been a cornerstone of his investment philosophy,

emphasizing the value of simplicity and financial prudence.

2. **Restraining Improper Thoughts and Actions - The Hershey Company**: The Hershey Company has long been committed to an ethical business model, prominently displayed in their sourcing of fair-trade ingredients. This commitment reflects their dedication to restraining from practices that could harm the environment or exploit labor, thereby maintaining a respected and ethical business standing.

3. **Avoiding Overindulgence - J.K. Rowling**: J.K. Rowling's journey from living on state benefits to becoming one of the world's best-selling authors exemplifies avoiding overindulgence. Despite her vast wealth, Rowling is known for her charitable giving and

modest living, focusing on using her resources to help others.

4. **Broadening Knowledge - Elon Musk**: Elon Musk's pursuit of broad knowledge across different scientific domains, from rocket science to artificial intelligence, underlines the importance of lifelong learning. His ventures, such as SpaceX and Tesla, showcase how extensive learning and curiosity can drive innovation and success.

5. **Maintaining High Moral Conduct - Patagonia**: Patagonia, the outdoor clothing brand, is an exemplar of maintaining high moral conduct in business operations. Their commitment to environmental sustainability and ethical labor practices demonstrates their dedication to refining their character as a

corporation, influencing the industry, and inspiring customers.

6. **Practicing Humility and Restraint - Angela Merkel**: Angela Merkel, the former Chancellor of Germany, is widely admired for her humility and restraint in leadership. Her approach to governance, characterized by calmness, prudence, and consideration, highlights the effectiveness of these virtues in achieving long-term, sustainable success and respect on the global stage.

These examples underscore the chapter's themes by showing how individuals and organizations embody the principles of self-discipline, ethical behavior, and continuous learning to achieve their aspirations and influence others positively.

Fundamental Virtue and Following the Way Chapter Four

Translation

The method of nurturing aspirations and practicing resolute action begins with the following principles:

Comprehensive Planning: There is no greater foundation than thorough deliberation.

Endurance: There is no greater stability than bearing insults with patience.

Cultivating Virtue: There is no greater priority than self-improvement through moral refinement.

Finding Joy in Goodness: There is no greater happiness than delighting in virtuous deeds.

Sincerity: There is no greater mystique than achieving absolute authenticity.

Understanding Nature: There is no greater clarity than grasping the essence of all things.

Contentment: There is no greater fortune than understanding when enough is enough.

On the other hand:

Excessive Desire: There is no greater suffering than harboring too many wishes.

Scattered Focus: There is no greater sorrow than a distracted mind.

Inconsistency: There is no greater illness than lack of steadiness.

Shortsightedness: There is no greater weakness than pursuing gains without foresight.

Greed and Pettiness: There is no greater obscurity than being consumed by trivialities.

Self-Reliance Without Support: There is no greater isolation than depending solely on oneself.

Doubt and Distrust: There is no greater danger than suspecting everything and everyone.

Selfishness: There is no greater downfall than being motivated by personal interests alone.

Summary of Chapter Four:

Fundamental Virtue and

Following the Way

This chapter explores the principles of nurturing aspirations and taking decisive actions through the cultivation of virtues and alignment with the Way (道). It contrasts the virtues that lead to happiness and success with the flaws that result in suffering and failure, providing a guide for achieving clarity, contentment, and fulfillment.

1. The Pillars of Virtue and Fulfillment:

Comprehensive Planning: Success begins with thoughtful deliberation and thorough preparation.

Endurance: Patience and the ability to endure insults bring stability and resilience.

Cultivating Virtue: Moral refinement and self-improvement are the highest priorities.

Finding Joy in Goodness: True happiness arises from delighting in virtuous deeds.

Sincerity: Absolute authenticity is a profound and transformative virtue.

Understanding Nature: Clarity comes from grasping the essence of all things.

Contentment: Recognizing when enough is enough is the greatest form of fortune.

2. The Pitfalls of Vice and Weakness:

Excessive Desire: Harboring too many wishes results in suffering.

Scattered Focus: A distracted mind leads to sorrow and inefficiency.

Inconsistency: A lack of steadiness undermines growth and success.

Shortsightedness: Pursuing immediate gains without foresight is a critical weakness.

Greed and Pettiness: Obsessing over trivialities clouds judgment and diminishes purpose.

Self-Reliance Without Support: Depending solely on oneself creates isolation and vulnerability.

Doubt and Distrust: Suspicion of everything and everyone brings danger and instability.

Selfishness: Acting out of personal interest alone is the greatest path to downfall.

Central Message

Chapter Four emphasizes the importance of cultivating virtues such as patience, sincerity, and contentment to align with the Way and achieve fulfillment. It contrasts these qualities with the detrimental effects of vices like greed, shortsightedness, and selfishness, which lead to suffering and isolation. By adhering to these principles, individuals can find clarity, stability, and success while avoiding the pitfalls of moral and mental imbalance.

Samples

"Fundamental Virtue and Following the Way" delves into the essential virtues that underpin a fulfilling and impactful life. This chapter showcases individuals and organizations that embody these virtues, providing a roadmap for readers on how to integrate these principles into their own lives to navigate complexities with moral clarity and achieve sustainable success.

1. **Comprehensive Planning - Sundar Pichai and Google**: Under Sundar Pichai's leadership, Google has excelled in comprehensive planning, particularly in its strategic approach to innovation and market expansion. Pichai's foresight in diversifying Google's product offerings–from AI technology to cloud computing–demonstrates the foundational virtue of thorough deliberation leading to stability and growth.

2. **Endurance - Nelson Mandela**: Nelson Mandela's life exemplifies endurance, particularly his capacity to bear insults and hardships with patience during his 27 years in prison. His resilience contributed to his effectiveness as a leader who steered South Africa

through its transition from apartheid to a democratic society.

3. **Cultivating Virtue - Oprah Winfrey**: Oprah Winfrey has consistently prioritized self-improvement and moral refinement, using her platform to promote educational initiatives, personal development, and philanthropy. Her dedication to cultivating virtue has made her a global symbol of integrity and benevolence.

4. **Finding Joy in Goodness - The LEGO Group**: The LEGO Group's corporate philosophy of 'Only the best is good enough' reflects a deep-seated commitment to delighting in virtuous deeds, particularly in their products' educational value and their sustainable practices. This approach has solidified LEGO's

reputation as a responsible and beloved brand.

5. **Sincerity - Sheryl Sandberg**: Sheryl Sandberg, through her work at Facebook and her book *Lean In*, advocates for sincerity in professional and personal life. Her commitment to authentic communication and leadership helps inspire women globally to achieve their full potential while fostering a culture of transparency in the workplace.

6. **Understanding Nature - Jane Goodall**: Renowned for her revolutionary studies on chimpanzees, Jane Goodall's deep understanding of nature and commitment to conservation teaches us the importance of connecting with and preserving our environment. Her work emphasizes the virtue of grasping the essence of all living things to

promote ecological balance and sustainability.

These examples serve as powerful illustrations of how fundamental virtues can guide individuals and organizations toward ethical practices and significant achievements. By aligning actions with virtues, the figures and companies mentioned in this chapter demonstrate the potential for profound impacts on society and personal fulfillment.

Upholding Righteousness Chapter Five

A leader who uses clarity to guide subordinates will not lead them into confusion.

A person unaware of their faults will inevitably encounter problems.

Those who stray but do not return to the correct path are lost.

Speaking in a way that provokes resentment invites disaster.

Issuing commands that conflict with one's intentions leads to failure.

Contradictory instructions undermine trust and destroy credibility.

Anger without dignity invites defiance.

Criticizing others harshly without regard for their dignity leads to misfortune.

Publicly shaming trusted individuals creates danger.

Disrespecting those who deserve reverence breeds misfortune.

Aligning outward appearances with insincere intentions leads to isolation.

Favoring slanderous individuals over loyal advisors leads to destruction.

Prioritizing indulgence over wisdom leads to ignorance.

Allowing personal relationships to interfere with public responsibilities leads to chaos.

Giving power to unworthy individuals creates instability.

Seeking victory through oppression results in hostility.

When reputation exceeds substance, losses occur.

Blaming others while ignoring one's own faults leads to failure.

Expecting much while giving little invites disappointment.

Disregarding the past achievements of others while clinging to old grievances leads to ruin.

Relying on individuals without principles results in betrayal.

Punishing without cause incites rebellion.

Rewarding undeservedly diminishes authority.

Listening to flattery while resenting honest advice leads to downfall.

Those who respect what they have achieve peace.

Those who covet what belongs to others cause destruction.

Summary of Chapter Five:

Upholding Righteousness

This chapter provides a comprehensive guide for maintaining righteousness in leadership and personal conduct, emphasizing the importance of clarity, fairness, and consistency. It warns against actions that undermine trust, credibility, and stability, offering insights into how leaders and individuals can uphold principles to avoid chaos and achieve harmony.

1. The Importance of Clarity and
   Integrity:

Leaders must use clarity to guide
subordinates, ensuring they are not led
into confusion.

Consistency between actions and
intentions builds trust, while
contradictions and insincerity lead to
isolation and failure.

Aligning words and deeds is essential to
maintain credibility and authority.

2. Avoiding Harmful Behaviors:

Anger without dignity invites defiance,
while harsh criticism and public
shaming breed resentment and danger.

Favoring slanderers over loyal advisors
or allowing indulgence to overshadow
wisdom creates instability and
ignorance.

Misusing power, whether by promoting unworthy individuals or rewarding undeservedly, leads to chaos and diminished respect.

3. The Consequences of Ignorance and Arrogance:

Leaders who fail to acknowledge their own faults, rely on unprincipled individuals, or ignore past achievements invite betrayal and ruin.

Seeking victory through oppression fosters hostility, while disregarding honest advice in favor of flattery accelerates downfall.

Excessive ambition and coveting what belongs to others destroy peace and stability.

4. Principles for Harmony and Success:

Respecting what one has and maintaining fairness fosters peace and harmony.

Avoiding unnecessary punishment, valuing dignity, and balancing expectations with contributions build trust and loyalty.

Acknowledging the accomplishments of others and fostering wisdom over indulgence create lasting success.

Central Message

Chapter Five emphasizes that righteousness is the foundation of trust, stability, and effective leadership. Leaders must act with clarity, fairness, and consistency, avoiding behaviors that breed resentment, instability, and failure. By upholding principles and respecting others, individuals and leaders alike can create harmony, achieve success, and maintain lasting peace.

Samples

"Upholding Righteousness" emphasizes the critical role of ethical integrity and fairness in leadership and personal conduct. This chapter presents examples of those who have exemplified these qualities, demonstrating how upholding righteousness can lead to trust, credibility, and lasting impact in various sectors of society.

1. **Clarity in Leadership - Satya Nadella, Microsoft**: Since taking over as CEO, Satya Nadella has revitalized Microsoft with a clear focus on integrity, innovation, and inclusivity. His leadership in transitioning Microsoft towards cloud computing and ethical AI demonstrates how clarity and ethical conduct can rejuvenate a company and lead it to new heights of success.

2. **Maintaining Integrity - Ruth Bader Ginsburg**: The late U.S. Supreme Court Justice Ruth Bader Ginsburg was renowned for her unwavering integrity and dedication to justice. Her career was marked by a consistent commitment to upholding the law and fighting for gender equality, making her a symbol of righteousness in the judicial world.

3. **Consistency and Fairness - Howard Schultz, Starbucks**: Howard Schultz's decision to provide comprehensive health benefits and stock options to both part-time and full-time employees at Starbucks set a new standard for fairness in the retail industry. His leadership demonstrates the importance of consistency and fairness in creating loyalty and trust among employees.

4. **Trustworthiness in Agreements - The Body Shop**: Founded by Anita Roddick, The Body Shop was one of the first companies to promote ethical consumerism. The brand's commitment to fair trade and opposition to animal testing pioneered standards for corporate social responsibility, showing how trustworthiness in agreements with consumers and suppliers can build a powerful and respected brand identity.

5. **Ethical Decision Making - Paul Polman, Unilever**: Paul Polman, former CEO of Unilever, redefined the company's strategy to focus on sustainability and ethical sourcing. His leadership not only enhanced Unilever's market position but also proved that ethical decision-making in business could lead to better

outcomes for both the company and the community.

These examples illustrate how upholding righteousness is not just about avoiding wrongdoing, but actively seeking to do right by stakeholders, the community, and the environment. Each example shows that ethical leadership is not only morally correct but also pragmatically effective in building sustainable success.

Harmonizing with Propriety Chapter Six

Resentment arises from not letting go of small faults.

Troubles emerge from failing to plan ahead.

Blessings come from accumulating goodness; disasters arise from accumulating evil.

Hunger results from neglecting agriculture; cold results from idleness in weaving.

Stability comes from having capable people; danger comes from mishandling matters.

Wealth is born from seizing opportunities; poverty comes from wasting them.

A ruler's constant impulsiveness creates chaos; subjects filled with doubt lack trust.

Disrespect for superiors leads to offenses; scorn for subordinates fosters alienation.

Close advisors who are not valued lead distant advisors to lose respect.

Those who distrust themselves fail to trust others; those who are self-assured do not doubt others.

A crooked ruler will have no upright officials; a biased superior will have no just subordinates.

A nation on the brink of ruin has no virtuous people; a government in disorder has no good individuals.

Those who deeply love their people will urgently seek virtuous talent.

A nation heading for greatness attracts people of worth; a state nearing collapse drives them away.

Land that is barren does not yield great harvests; shallow waters cannot support large fish.

Bald trees do not attract large birds; sparse forests do not shelter great beasts.

Steep mountains crumble; full lakes overflow.

Discarding jade for stones reveals blindness; adorning oneself with false strength invites ridicule.

Clothes worn improperly result in disgrace; walking without looking at the ground leads to falls.

Weak pillars cause buildings to collapse; weak support causes nations to fall.

Cold feet affect the heart; discontent among the people harms the nation.

Mountains that are about to collapse first show signs of instability; nations that are in decline first reveal the exhaustion of their people.

Withering roots and decayed branches signify the ruin of people and nations.

A cart on the same path as an overturned one will tip; a nation repeating the mistakes of a failed one will perish.

Witnessing others' failures should inspire caution; seeing their tracks should encourage avoidance.

Fear of danger ensures safety; fear of ruin ensures survival.

The actions of people, when aligned with the Way, bring blessings; when contrary to the Way, bring misfortune.

Those who pursue goodness face no evil; those who lack foresight encounter near-term troubles.

Like attracts like: those with shared goals find each other, those with shared virtues support each other, those with shared evils band together, and those with shared loves seek each other.

Aligning with the correct principles harmonizes individuals, families, and nations. Those who act contrary to the principles invite disorder; those who follow them create order.

Summary of Chapter Six:

Harmonizing with Propriety

This chapter emphasizes the importance of aligning with propriety and universal principles to achieve harmony within individuals, families, and nations. It explores how virtues, planning, and foresight bring blessings, while impulsiveness, negligence, and discord lead to misfortune and ruin. The chapter uses vivid metaphors and examples to highlight the causes and consequences of harmony and disorder.

1. The Roots of Harmony and Disorder:

Harmony arises from accumulating goodness, respecting others, and planning ahead. In contrast, resentment, trouble, and disasters result from clinging to faults, neglecting responsibilities, and indulging in impulsive actions.

Stability and wealth stem from capable individuals and seizing opportunities, while danger and poverty arise from mishandling matters and wasting resources.

2. Leadership and Governance:

A ruler's impulsiveness and mistrust sow chaos, while disrespect for superiors and scorn for subordinates alienate people and erode trust.

A just and virtuous government attracts capable individuals and ensures national prosperity, while a biased and corrupt administration leads to the nation's decline.

3. Lessons from Nature and History:

Natural metaphors illustrate the consequences of imbalance: barren land yields no harvest, shallow waters cannot support life, and crumbling mountains forewarn of collapse.

Nations repeat the mistakes of failed predecessors when they fail to learn from history. Observing others' failures should inspire caution and encourage avoidance of similar paths.

4. The Importance of Alignment with the Way:

Acting in accordance with the Way brings blessings, while straying from it invites misfortune. Shared virtues and values harmonize individuals and societies, while misalignment fosters discord and chaos.

Fear of danger promotes safety, and adherence to goodness ensures resilience against evil.

Central Message

Chapter Six underscores that harmony within oneself, relationships, and governance is achieved through virtue, propriety, and alignment with universal principles. Neglecting these principles leads to instability and ruin, while respecting them ensures order, prosperity, and safety. By learning from history, avoiding impulsiveness, and fostering goodness, individuals and nations can thrive.

Samples

"Harmonizing with Propriety" explores the critical role of respect, tradition, and proper conduct in achieving harmony within organizations and societies. This chapter showcases how individuals and businesses that adhere to these principles can foster stable, respectful, and successful environments. Here, we illustrate how aligning actions with cultural and ethical expectations promotes lasting success and community well-being.

1. **Respecting Traditions - The Toyota Way**: Toyota is renowned for its corporate culture, which emphasizes respect for people and continuous improvement, known as 'The Toyota Way'. This philosophy is deeply rooted in the Japanese tradition of craftsmanship and propriety, leading to high quality, efficiency, and employee satisfaction, illustrating the benefits of harmonizing business practices with cultural propriety.

2. **Maintaining Social Order - Angela Merkel**: As Chancellor of Germany, Angela Merkel demonstrated the importance of propriety in leadership during crises, such as the Eurozone and refugee situations. Her ability to

uphold dignity and calmness, respecting both German norms and European Union protocols, helped maintain social and political order during turbulent times.

3. **Promoting Ethical Interactions - Patagonia:** Patagonia's commitment to environmental ethics extends beyond its products to how it interacts with customers and suppliers. The company's transparent supply chain practices and its advocacy for environmental causes demonstrate how businesses can lead in promoting ethical interactions and sustainability, aligning with societal values of propriety and responsibility.

4. **Cultural Respect in Global Operations - Netflix:** As Netflix expands globally, it has made significant efforts to respect and

incorporate local cultures into its offerings. By producing region-specific content and respecting local propriety norms, Netflix has successfully entered diverse markets, showing that cultural respect is key to international business success.

5. **Advocating for Proper Conduct - Malala Yousafzai**: Malala Yousafzai's advocacy for girls' education worldwide respects and promotes the propriety of learning and enlightenment across different cultures. Her work not only champions education but also encourages societies to align with the propriety of respecting human rights and promoting gender equality.

These examples from diverse fields and backgrounds illustrate the power of propriety in fostering respect, efficiency, and ethical behavior. By adhering to the principles of propriety, individuals and organizations can achieve greater harmony and success, providing valuable lessons for readers on how to integrate these principles into their own lives and work.

The Full Chinese Original Book

For your convenience, I attached the Chinese original book Sushu for people who know's Chinese Character or after a while you will know all the these 1360 characters. The next page will be the full Chinese book SuShu in Simplified Chinese. Yes, that's correct, only one page.

素书

原始章第一

夫道、德、仁、义、礼，五者一体也。道者，人之所蹈，使万物不知其所由；德者，人之所得，使万物各得其所欲；仁者，人之所亲，有慈惠恻隐之心，以遂其生成；义者，人之所宜，赏善罚恶，以立功立事；礼者，人之所履，夙兴夜寐，以成人伦之序。夫欲为人之本，不可无一焉。贤人君子明于盛衰之道，通乎成败之数，审乎治乱之势，达乎去就之理，故潜居抱道，以待其时。若时至而行，则能极人臣之位；得机而动，则能成绝代之功。如其不遇，没身而已。是以其道足高，而名重于后代。

正道章第二

德足以怀远，信足以一异，义足以得众，才足以鉴古，明足以照下，此人之俊也。行足以为仪表，智足以决嫌疑，信足以使守约，廉足以使分财，此人之豪也。守职而不废，处义而不回，见嫌而不苟免，见利而不苟得，此人之杰也。

求人之志章第三

绝嗜禁欲，所以除累；抑非损恶，所以禳过；贬酒阙色，所以无污；避嫌远疑，所以不误；博学切问，所以广知；高行微言，所以修身；恭俭谦约，所以自守；深计远虑，所以不穷；亲仁友直，所以扶颠；近恕笃行，所以接人；任材使能，所以济务；瘅恶斥谗，所以止乱；推古验今，所以不惑；先揆后度，所以应卒；设变致权，所以解结；括囊顺会，所以无咎；橛橛梗梗，所以立功；孜孜淑淑，所以保终。

本德宗道章第四

夫志心笃行之术，长莫长于博谋，安莫安于忍辱，先莫先于修德，乐莫乐于好善，神莫神于至诚，明莫明于体物；吉莫吉于知足，苦莫苦于多愿，悲莫悲于精散，病莫病于无常，短莫短于苟得，幽莫幽于贪鄙，孤莫孤于自恃，危莫危于任疑，败莫败于多私。

遵义章第五

以明示下者暗，有过不知者蔽，迷而不返者惑，以言取怨者祸，令过心乖者废，后令谬前者毁，怒而无威者犯，好直辱人者殃，戮辱所任者危，慢其所敬者凶，貌合心离者孤，亲谗远忠者亡，近色远贤者惛，女谒公行者乱，私人以官者浮，凌下取胜者侵，名不胜实者耗，略己而责人者不治，自厚而薄人者弃，以过弃功者损，群下外异者沦，既用不任者疏，行赏吝色者沮，多许少与者怨，既迎而拒者乖，薄施厚望者不报，贵而忘贱者不久，念旧而弃新功者凶，用人不得正者殆，强用人者不畜，为人择官者乱，失其所强者弱，决策于不仁者险，阴计外泄者败，厚敛薄施者凋。战士贫、游士富者衰，货赂公行者昧，闻善忽略、记过不忘者暴，所任不可信，所信不可任者浊，牧人以德者集，绳人以刑者散。小功不赏，则大功不立，小怨不赦，则大怨必生。赏不服人，罚不甘心者叛，赏及无功，罚及无罪者酷。听谗而美、闻谏而仇者亡。能有其有者安，贪人之有者残。

安礼章第六

怨在不舍小过，患在不预定谋。福在积善，祸在积恶，饥在贱农，寒在惰织，安在得人，危在失事。富在迎来，贫在弃时。上无常躁，下无疑心。轻上生罪，侮下无亲。近臣不重，远臣轻之。自疑不信人，自信不疑人。枉士无正友，曲上无直下，危国无贤人，乱政无善人。爱人深者求贤急，乐得贤者养人厚。国乱霸者士皆归，邦将亡者贤先避。地薄者大物不产，水浅者大物不游，树秃者大禽不栖，林疏者大兽不居。山峭者崩，泽满者溢。弃玉取石者盲，羊质虎皮者辱。衣不举领者倒，走不视地者颠。柱弱者屋坏，辅弱者国倾。足寒伤心，人怨伤国。山将崩者下先隳，国将衰者人先弊。根枯枝朽，人困国残。与覆车同轨者倾，与亡国同事者灭。见已生者慎将生，恶其迹者须避之。畏危者安，畏亡者存。夫人之所行，有道则吉，无道则凶。吉者百福所归，凶者百祸所攻，非其神圣，自然所钟。务善策者无恶事，无远虑者有近忧。同志相得，同仁相忧，同恶相党，同爱相求，同美相妒，同智相谋，同贵相害，同利相忌，同声相应，同气相感，同类相依，同义相亲，同难相济，同道相成，同艺相规，同巧相胜，此乃数之所得，不可与理违。释己而教人者逆，正己而化人者顺，逆者难从，顺者易行，难从则乱，易行则理。如此，理身、理家、理国，可也。

The Full Original Chinese Book With PinYin For Reading

For your convenience, I attached the PinYin version for people are not very familiar with the pronunciation of the Chinese Characters . The following 8 pages are the full Chinese Book SuShu with PinYin.

原始章第一

fū dào、dé、rén、yì、lǐ，wǔ zhě yì tǐ yě。

夫道、德、仁、义、礼，五者一体也。

dào zhě，rén zhī suǒ dǎo，shǐ wàn wù bù zhī qí suǒ yóu。

道者，人之所蹈，使万物不知其所由。

dé zhě，rén zhī suǒ dé，shǐ wàn wù gè dé qí suǒ yù。

德者，人之所得，使万物各得其所欲。

rén zhě，rén zhī suǒ qīn，yǒu cí huì cè yǐn zhī xīn，yǐ suì qí shēng chéng。

仁者，人之所亲，有慈惠恻隐之心，以遂其生成。

yì zhě，rén zhī suǒ yí，shǎng shàn fá è，yǐ lì gōng lì shì。

义者，人之所宜，赏善罚恶，以立功立事。

lǐ zhě，rén zhī suǒ lǚ，sù xīng yè mèi，yǐ chéng rén lún zhī xù。

礼者，人之所履，夙兴夜寐，以成人伦之序。

fū yù wéi rén zhī běn，bù kě wú yī yān。

夫欲为人之本，不可无一焉。

xián rén jūn zǐ，míng yú shèng shuāi zhī dào，

贤人君子，明于盛衰之道，

tōng hū chéng bài zhī shù，shěn hū zhì luàn zhī shì，dá hū qù jiù zhī lǐ。

通乎成败之数，审乎治乱之势，达乎去就之理。

gù qián jū bào dào，yǐ dài qí shí。

故潜居抱道，以待其时。

ruò shí zhì ér xíng，zé néng jí rén chén zhī wèi；

若时至而行 ，则能极人臣之位；

dé jī ér dòng，zé néng chéng jué dài zhī gōng。

得机而动，则能成绝代之功。

rú qí bù yù ，mò shēn ér yǐ。

如其不遇，没身而已。

shì yǐ qí dào zú gāo，ér míng zhòng yú hòu dài。

是以其道足高，而名重于后代。

正道章第二

dé zú yǐ huái yuǎn， xìn zú yǐ yī yì。

德足以怀远 ，信足以一异，

yì zú yǐ dé zhòng，cái zú yǐ jiàn gǔ，míng zú yǐ zhào xià，cǐ rén zhī jùn yě。

义足以得众，才足以鉴古，明足以照下，此人之俊也！

xíng zú yǐ wéi yí biǎo, zhì zú yǐ jué xián yí.

行足以为仪表，智足以决嫌疑，

xìn kě yǐ shǐ shǒu yuē lián kě yǐ shǐ fēn cái cǐ rén zhī hǎo yě。

信可以使守约，廉可以使分财，此人之豪也！

shǒu zhí ér bù fèi，chù yì ér bù huí，

守职而不废，处义而不回，

jiàn xián ér bù gǒu miǎn，jiàn lì ér bù gǒu dé，cǐ rén zhī jié yě！

见嫌而不苟免，见利而不苟得，此人之杰也！

求人之志章第三

jué shì jìn yù，suǒ yǐ chú lèi。yì fēi sǔn è，suǒ yǐ ràng guò。biǎn jiǔ què sè，suǒ yǐ wú wū。

绝嗜禁欲，所以除累。抑非损恶，所以禳过。贬酒阙色，所以无污。

bì xián yuǎn yí，suǒ yǐ bù wù。bó xué qiē wèn，suǒ yǐ guǎng zhī。gāo xíng wēi yán，suǒ yǐ xiū shēn。

避嫌远疑，所以不误。博学切问，所以广知。高行微言，所以修身。

gōng jiǎn qiān yuē，suǒ yǐ zì shǒu。shēn jì yuǎn lǜ，suǒ yǐ bù qióng。

恭俭谦约，所以自守。深计远虑，所以不穷。

qīn rén yǒu zhí， suǒ yǐ fú diān。 jìn shù dǔ xíng，suǒ yǐ jiē rén。rèn cái shǐ néng ，suǒ yǐ jì wù。

亲仁友直，所以扶颠。近恕笃行 ，所以接人。任材使能 ，所以济物。

dān è chì chán， suǒ yǐ zhǐ luàn。tuī gǔ yàn jīn，suǒ yǐ bù huò。xiān kuí hòu dù，suǒ yǐ yìng zú。

殚恶斥谗 ，所以止乱。推古验今，所以不惑。先揆后度，所以应卒。

shè biàn zhì quán，suǒ yǐ jiě jié。kuò náng shùn huì，suǒ yǐ wú jiù。

设变致权 ，所以解结。括囊顺会，所以无咎。

jué jué gěng gěng，suǒ yǐ lì gōng。zī zī shū shū suǒ yǐ bǎo zhōng。

橛橛梗梗 ，所以立功。孜孜淑淑，所以保终 。

本德宗道章第四

fū zhì xīn dǔ xíng zhī shù：

夫志心笃行之术：

cháng mò cháng yú bó móu，ān mò ān yú rěn rǔ。xiān mò xiān yú xiū dé，lè mò lè yú hào shàn。

长莫长于博谋，安莫安于忍辱，先莫先于修德，乐莫乐于好善 ，

shén mò shén yú zhì chéng，míng mò míng yú tǐ wù，jí mò jí yú zhī zú。

神莫神于至诚 ，明莫明于体物，吉莫吉于知足。

kǔ mò kǔ yú duō yuàn，bēi mò bēi yú jīng sàn。bìng mò bìng yú wú cháng，duǎn mò duǎn yú gǒu dé。

苦莫苦于多愿 ，悲莫悲于精散，病莫病于无常，短莫短于苟得，

yōu mò yōu yú tān bǐ，gū mò gū yú zì shì，wēi mò wēi yú rèn yí， bài mò bài yú duō sī。

幽莫幽于贪鄙，孤莫孤于自恃，危莫危于任疑，败莫败于多私。

遵义章第五

yǐ míng shì xià zhě àn，yǒu guò bù zhī zhě bì，mí ér bù fǎn zhě huò，yǐ yán qǔ yuàn zhě huò，

以明示下者暗，有过不知者蔽，迷而不返者惑，以言取怨者祸，

lìng yǔ xīn guāi zhě fèi，hòu lìng miù qián zhě huǐ，nù ér wú wēi zhě fàn，hǎo zhòng rǔ rén zhě yāng，

令与心乖者废，后令谬前者毁，怒而无威者犯，好众辱人者殃 ，

lù rǔ suǒ rèn zhě wēi，màn qí suǒ jìng zhě xiōng，mào hé xīn lí zhě gū，qīn chán yuǎn zhōng zhě wáng，

戮辱所任者危，慢其所敬者凶 ，貌合心离者孤，亲谗远忠者亡 ，

jìn sè yuǎn xián zhě hūn，nǚ yè gōng xíng zhě luàn，sī rén yǐ guān zhě fú，líng xià qǔ shèng zhě qīn，

近色远贤者昏，女谒公行者乱，私人以官者浮，凌下取胜者侵，

míng bú shèng shí zhě hào。lüè jǐ ér zé rén zhě bù zhì， zì hòu ér báo rén zhě qì fèi。

名不胜实者耗。略己而责人者不治，自厚而薄人者弃废。

yǐ guò qì gōng zhě sǔn，qún xià wài yì zhě lún，jì yòng bù rèn zhě shū。

以过弃功者损，群下外异者沦，既用不任者疏。

xíng shǎng lìn sè zhě jǔ，duō xǔ shǎo yǔ zhě yuàn，jì yíng ér jù zhě guāi。

行赏吝色者沮，多许少与者怨，既迎而拒者乖。

báo shī hòu wàng zhě bù bào，guì ér wàng jiàn zhě bù jiǔ。niàn jiù ér qì xīn gōng zhě xiōng，

薄施厚望者不报，贵而忘贱者不久。念旧而弃新功者凶，

yòng rén bù zhèng zhě dài, qiáng yòng rén zhě bù chù, wéi rén zé guān zhě luàn,

用人不正者殆，强用人者不畜，为人择官者乱，

shī qí suǒ qiáng zhě ruò, jué cè yú bù rén zhě xiǎn, yīn jì wài xiè zhě bài, hòu liǎn báo shī zhě diāo。

失其所强者弱，决策于不仁者险，阴计外泄者败，厚敛薄施者凋。

zhàn shì pín,yóu shì fù zhě shuāi ,huò lù gōng xíng zhě mèi,wén shàn hū lüè, jì guò bù wàng zhě bào;

战士贫，游士富者衰；货赂公行者昧，闻善忽略，记过不忘者暴；

suǒ rèn bù kě xìn, suǒ xìn bù kě rèn zhě zhuó。mù rén yǐ dé zhě jí, shéng rén yǐ xíng zhě sàn。

所任不可信，所信不可任者浊。牧人以德者集，绳人以刑者散。

xiǎo gōng bù shǎng, zé dà gōng bù lì; xiǎo yuàn bù shè, zé dà yuàn bì shēng。

小功不赏，则大功不立；小怨不赦，则大怨必生。

shǎng bù fú rén, fá bù gān xīn zhě pàn。shǎng jí wú gōng, fá jí wú zuì zhě kù。

赏不服人，罚不甘心者叛。赏及无功，罚及无罪者酷。

tīng chán ér měi, wén jiàn ér chóu zhě wáng。néng yǒu qí yǒu zhě ān, tān rén zhī yǒu zhě cán。

听谗而美，闻谏而仇者亡。能有其有者安，贪人之有者残。

安礼章第六

yuàn zài bù shě xiǎo guò, huàn zài bù yù dìng móu。fú zài jǐ shàn, huò zài jǐ è。

怨在不舍小过，患在不预定谋。福在积善，祸在积恶。

jǐ zài jiàn nóng, hán zài duò zhī。ān zài dé rén, wēi zài shī shì。fù zài yíng lái, pín zài qì shí。

饥在贱农，寒在堕织。安在得人，危在失事。富在迎来，贫在弃时。

shàng wú cháng cāo, xià duō yí xīn。qīng shàng shēng zuì，rǔ xià wú qīn。

上无常操，下多疑心。轻上生罪，侮下无亲。

jìn chén bù zhòng，yuǎn chén qīng zhī。zì yí bù xìn rén，zì xìn bù yí rén。

近臣不重，远臣轻之。自疑不信人，自信不疑人。

wǎng shì wú zhèng yǒu，qū shàng wú zhí xià。wēi guó wú xián rén，luàn zhèng wú shàn rén。

枉士无正友，曲上无直下。危国无贤人，乱政无善人。

ài rén shēn zhě qiú xián jí，lè dé xián zhě yǎng rén hòu。

爱人深者求贤急，乐得贤者养人厚。

guó jiāng bà zhě shì jiē guī，bāng jiāng wáng zhě xián xiān bì。

国将霸者士皆归，邦将亡者贤先避。

dì báo zhě dà wù bù chǎn，shuǐ qiǎn zhě dà yú bù yóu，

地薄者大物不产，水浅者大鱼不游，

shù tū zhě dà qín bù qī，lín shū zhě dà shòu bù jū。

树秃者大禽不栖，林疏者大兽不居。

shān qiào zhě bēng，zé mǎn zhě yì。qì yù qǔ shí zhě máng，yáng zhì hǔ pí zhě róu。

山峭者崩，泽满者溢。弃玉取石者盲，羊质虎皮者柔。

yī bù jǔ lǐng zhě dǎo，zǒu bù shì dì zhě diān。zhù ruò zhě wū huài，fǔ ruò zhě guó qīng。

衣不举领者倒，走不视地者颠。柱弱者屋坏，辅弱者国倾。

zú hán shāng xīn，mín yuàn shāng guó。shān jiāng bēng zhě xià xiān huī；

足寒伤心，民怨伤国。山将崩者下先隳；

guó jiāng shuāi zhě，mín xiān bì，gēn kū zhī xiǔ，mín kùn guó cán。

国将衰者，民先敝，根枯枝朽，民困国残。

国将衰者，民先毙。根枯枝朽，民困国残。

yǔ fù chē tóng guǐ zhě qīng，yǔ wáng guó tóng shì zhě miè。

与覆车同轨者倾，与亡国同事者灭。

jiàn yǐ shēng zhě shèn jiāng shī；è qí jì zhě，xū bì zhī。wèi wēi zhě ān，wèi wáng zhě cún，

见已生者，慎将失；恶其迹者，须避之。畏危者安，畏亡者存。

fū rén zhī suǒ xíng：yǒu dào zé jí，wú dào zé xiōng。

夫人之所行：有道则吉，无道则凶。

jí zhě bǎi fú suǒ guī，xiōng zhě bǎi huò suǒ gōng。fēi qí shén shèng，zì rán suǒ zhōng。

吉者百福所归，凶者百祸所攻。非其神圣，自然所钟。

wù shàn cè zhě，wú è shì；wú yuǎn lǜ zhě，yǒu jìn yōu。

务善策者，无恶事；无远虑者，有近忧。

tóng zhì xiāng dé，tóng rén xiāng yōu，tóng è xiāng dǎng，tóng ài xiāng qiú，

同志相得，同仁相忧，同恶相党，同爱相求，

tóng měi xiāng dù，tóng zhì xiāng móu，tóng guì xiāng hài，tóng lì xiāng jì，

同美相妒，同智相谋，同贵相害，同利相忌，

tóng shēng xiāng yìng，tóng qì xiāng gǎn。tóng lèi xiāng yī，tóng yì xiāng qīn，

同声相应，同气相感。同类相依，同义相亲，

tóng nàn xiāng jì，tóng dào xiāng chéng，tóng yì xiāng kuī，tóng qiǎo xiāng shèng，

同难相济，同道相成，同艺相窥，同巧相胜，

cǐ nǎi shù zhī suǒ dé，bù kě yǔ lǐ wéi。

此乃数之所得，不可与理违。

shì jǐ ér jiào rén zhě nì，zhèng jǐ ér huà rén zhě shùn。

释己而教人者逆，正己而化人者顺。

nì zhě nán cóng、shùn zhě yì xíng，nán cóng zé luàn，yì xíng zé lǐ。

逆者难从，顺者易行，难从则乱，易行则理。

rú cǐ， lǐ shēn、lǐ jiā、lǐ guó kě yě！

如此，理身、理家、理国可也！

About The Author

The origins of **"Su Shu"** are attributed to the legendary figure **Huang Shigong**, an enigmatic sage during the late Warring States period (475-221 BCE).

Huang Shigong is renowned for his profound knowledge of strategy, governance, and human nature. He is most famously associated with imparting his wisdom to Zhang Liang, a key strategist who played a pivotal role in the establishment of the Han Dynasty. "SuShu" is said to encapsulate the core teachings of Huang Shigong, emphasizing principles of leadership, morality, and strategic thinking.

The version of **"SuShu"** widely known today is linked to **Zhang Shangying**, a scholar and statesman of the Northern Song Dynasty (960-1127). Zhang Shangying is believed to have studied and refined the text, presenting it as a guide to ethical leadership and self-cultivation. His efforts helped preserve and promote the timeless wisdom of "SuShu" making it a cornerstone of Chinese philosophical and strategic literature.

About the Translator

Morning Lee, author of *Risk Free Startup Success* and translator of *From Leadership to Success: The Timeless Laws*, is deeply passionate about business, startups, and leadership. With extensive experience founding and managing ventures across industries such as shipping, moving, real estate, IT, trading, courier services, and furniture, Morning brings a wealth of practical knowledge to the table.

While the translation of *Su Shu* showcases Morning's appreciation for the profound wisdom of ancient Chinese philosophy, the focus remains on demonstrating how these timeless principles can be applied to modern business challenges. Through both original works and translations, Morning empowers readers with actionable insights to build successful ventures and thrive in the competitive world of entrepreneurship.

www.ingramcontent.com/pod-product-compliance
Lightning Source LLC
Chambersburg PA
CBHW030533210326
41597CB00014B/1133